I0540499

THE WHEEL OF NEEDS

Living life to the fullest

by

Bjørn Årstad Seyffarth

ISBN 978-82-690833-0-9 *(Printed)*

ISBN 978-82-690833-1-6 *(Electronic)*

TO LIVE LIFE FULLY

To live a life fully does not demand any explaining or justifying story; it does not demand a meaning of life. If our needs are met, life is beautiful and satisfying in itself.

What each of us needs to experience to live life fully is very different. However, if the seven basic needs are met, life would hardly seem meaningless!

Seen from another angle, we could say that each of these needs can be a fruitful starting point for enumerable possible stories that can fill the role as the meaning of life.

Many people live full and rich lives without having all their needs met. If we have bountifully fulfilled one or several of these needs it can be enough, especially if we adhere to a story that prescribes it to be so. For example, if love is overflowing in our family, among friends and even at work, other needs may be less important. Unmet needs do not necessarily mean that something is missing.

If the connection with the Whole, a higher calling, or God is compelling and all-consuming, many of the other needs may fall away.

It can be demanding to be involved in life, and we have limited time and energy. It can be necessary to focus on those needs that are most important to us and let the others be.

What each of us needs to feel fulfilled also varies greatly. Some people may have a dog or a cat and enjoy spending most of their time pottering about by themselves, while others feel the need to connect with many people, and achieve a lot, whether at work, at home with family or going out with friends.

The need for sexuality can be forsaken and sublimated for the sake of creativity and art, or for the love of God.

Power and influence can somewhat compensate for a basic sense of insecurity, but are not necessarily healthy substitutes.

Love, friendship and belonging are essential for our sense of living life fully, and therefore I made that piece of the pie bigger than the others.

The Wheel of Needs has certain features in common with Abraham Maslow's hierarchy of needs (1943), often presented as a pyramid. The reason I chose a wheel is to show that the needs are not necessarily building on each other like building blocks, where the first level is a prerequisite for the second level etc. I don't believe the needs influence each other only one way, from the bottom up, rather that they influence each other in several directions in a more complicated pattern.

For example, love gives us a greater sense of security. Greater security gives deeper intimacy in our sexuality and a healthier form of personal strength, which in turn makes greater love possible.

To express truthfully, creatively and spontaneously presupposes a certain sense of safety, but when we eventually muster the courage to express honestly, it gives us joy and self-love which in turn makes it possible to love others more fully.

Clarity and understanding enable us to make conscious choices, and can thereby enhance our personal power and influence.

Contact with a higher consciousness can enhance our clarity and sense of safety.

Everything is connected.

THE WHEEL OF NEEDS

Growing up, we all have our basic needs met to different degrees. Ideally, I would grow up:

• *Feeling safe*

• *Accepting and enjoying my body and its functions in physical closeness and in enjoyment of mother's milk and food*

• *Having my boundaries respected and my wishes taken into consideration*

• *Being loved and seen when happy, loved and seen when sad and loved and seen even when angry*

• *Having my truth valued, heard and taken into consideration*

• *Having my creativity and play encouraged and protected*

• *Having a clear understanding of my place and role in my family*

• *Feeling myself to be a natural part of the universe*

Growing up in such a way lays the foundation for a good relationship with myself as an adult. I already feel safe. I feel good about my body, and confident with physical closeness and sexuality. I feel strong and respect myself without the need for external confirmation. I feel that I am worthy of love because I love myself. I feel free to express my truth and creativity. I know who I am in relation to others. And I experience myself as a given part of the whole.

It seems that most of us received less than the whole lot as our foundation. **The Wheel of Needs** is meant as a tool to help understand where the possibilities for nourishment and growth lie. Understanding *your* wheel can point you toward what can be done to make your life fuller and richer.

The seven needs:

I. **Safety**: I have a need to feel safe

II. **Intimacy**: I have a need for intimacy and enjoyment of food and sex

III. **Strength**: I have a need to feel strong and capable

IV. **Love and belonging**: I have a need for love and belonging

V. **Expression**: I have a need to express myself truthfully, creatively, and spontaneously

VI. **Clarity**: I have a need to understand and to be awake and present in my life

VII. **Wholeness**: I have a need to feel connected with something greater than myself

You can evaluate to which degree each need is met in your life. All needs are not equally important to everyone – it depends on who you are and which story you live by.

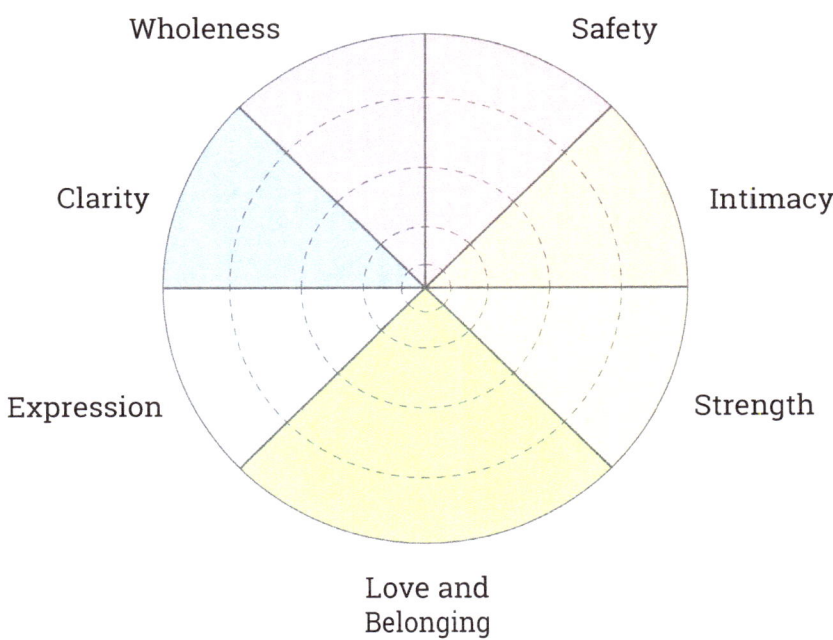

Evaluate each of the sentences on the next page according to the following scale:

5- this sentence is completely true for me
4- this sentence fits quite well for me
3- this sentence is partly true for me
2- this sentence is mostly untruth for me
1- this sentence is not true for me

I. Safety: I feel safe (Alternatively, how fully you evaluate this need to be met in your life)

II. Intimacy: I enjoy physical closeness, food and sexual interaction (Alternatively, how fully you evaluate this need to be met in your life)

III. Strength: I feel strong, I am in control of my life and I respect myself (Alternatively, how fully you evaluate this need to be met in your life)

IV. Love and belonging: My daily life is filled with friendship and love (Alternatively, how fully you evaluate this need to be met in your life)

V. Expression: I express myself truthfully and have outlet for my creativity and play (Alternatively, how fully you evaluate this need to be met in your life)

VI. Clarity: I understand myself and my environment, I am present in the moment and make conscious choices (Alternatively, how fully you evaluate this need to be met in your life)

VII.Wholeness: I feel myself to be connected to the Whole (Alternatively, how fully you evaluate this need to be met in your life)

When you have found the number for each sentence you can colour the wheel of needs to get a visual impression of which needs are met and which are not fully met. Colour each need with the corresponding colour. If your need is fully met, you select the number five and that piece of the pie is fully covered. If the need is not yet met it might warrant a one or a two and you will then fill in the first or the second ring of that piece of the pie and so on.

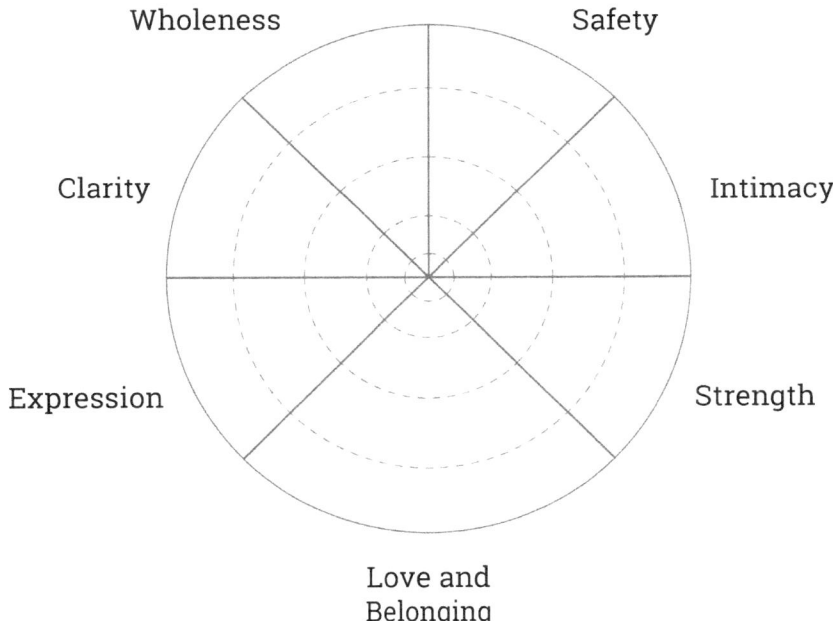

THINGS AND STUFF

I view these seven needs as subjective. That means that they naturally express themselves very differently from person to person, and quite independently of outside circumstances.

Some people seem to have everything externally, but still their most basic needs are not met. For example, we can imagine a man who has a well-paid job, a fancy car, a big house, and a holiday home, as well as a family, but he experiences alienation in relation to his co-workers, his wife and his children. This man is getting few of his needs met even though the facade looks good.

Others may have next to nothing but still experience a full and rich life. We can imagine a girl who grows up in a poor family where everybody takes care of each other. She does not have the same clothes or toys as other children, but she receives love and care from both her mother and her father. It is not easy to be poor, but when it comes down to it, the human connection is more fundamental for our life's experience and joy than material wealth.

THE FOUR STATES

---

1. Longing
2. Closed off
3. Fulfilled
4. Overflowing

Longing

When we are in contact with our needs, but remain unfulfilled, we experience longing - a longing often for a person or a thing that represents the fulfillment of that need for us. For example, as a man I dream of a woman that will fulfill my need for intimacy, sexuality and love.

When we believe a need can only be met in one specific way, for example, by a certain partner, a certain job, etc., we close off from other ways to fulfill that need which may be more accessible to us than we have allowed ourselves to take in.

Longing drives us forward, motivates us and inspires us to do the most incredible things. Some people claim that everything men do, they do to impress women! I think that diminishes who we are, because as men we also have other needs that do not involve women and vice versa. However, our longings to fulfill needs are strong forces and very possibly what drives our lives.

When we do something from longing, or give from longing, we give to get something back. We give to get:

- *Gratitude*
- *Recognition*
- *Respect*
- *Status*
- *Power*
- *Sex*
- *Self-worth*
- *Admiration etc.*

There is nothing wrong with giving from longing. It can be a beautiful mutual exchange. We give and we receive. Generosity is to give a little more than what we receive.

It can be hazardous to wake up and connect with a need that is not being fulfilled. We become painfully aware of what is missing in our life. This can lead to a depressive downward spiral. It demands strength and surplus energy to stay open in longing and remain hopeful and positive.

Longing is a movement away from what exists in this moment. This movement, this hope, makes us move forward, urges us to develop and experience something greater and more than what we live today. We reach a good balance when we have one foot firmly planted in gratitude for what we already have and one foot raised in the hope of something better.

Closed off

To stay put in a state of longing over an extended period of time is painful. Fortunately something in us closes off the contact with the need so we can still live quite contently. This is a good protection mechanism when the fulfillment of the need is not in sight. If we constantly feel into everything we don't have, we won't be very happy. To be closed gives us a certain stability and peace.

However, it can go so far that we are not at all in contact with our needs. We become numb. The advantage is that we are not torn by longing – the disadvantage is that we experience life as empty and meaningless. Thoughts churn around in our head, but we no longer have any connection with our emotions and needs.

When the connection with our needs is closed off, we live in a shadow world because the connection with the very pulse of life is closed off.

The needs can still exist strongly in us even when we are not conscious of them or in contact with them. They can be as black holes we don't see, but still influence our behaviour and how people see us (as in *Johari's Window*). These hidden needs show up as unconscious and often destructive behaviour.

Many people struggle with addiction, greed and obsessive desire. No matter how much they get, it is never enough. I believe these addictions originate in natural needs that were not fulfilled while growing up, or from these needs having been closed off or disconnected at some point in life.

This shadow side of a need can have an almost desperate pull to be fulfilled, but with something other than the basic need. Unconsciously we try to meet genuine needs with superficial substitutes. For example, we seek praise, admiration and attention instead of love. Or we crave ever more status, power and money instead of healing the need for inner safety and stability that might be the core issue. Other forms of addiction such as drugs, alcohol, sex, food, entertainment etc. are common expressions of shadow needs or needs out of balance.

I believe much will be healed if we meet our basic needs directly instead of with substitutes. That way the troublesome substitutes are no longer needed. When we see and acknowledge our problems, and the true needs they cover, we bring them out of the unconscious darkness into the light of awareness. Thereby we dramatically increase our chances of dealing with them rationally, that is, we can do something about our situation.

An example from my own life is about the need for strength. At a certain point in life I believed myself to be high above what I saw as a lowly need – the need for status and recognition from society. I mean, I was after all a spiritual person! Still I found myself fishing after compliments in almost every conversation that I had – mostly unconsciously. This need to be seen and accepted originated from my being unable to accept myself and my situation as good enough. I therefore needed other people´s approval and recognition to convince me that I was OK.

My job as a teacher for *Leadership by Heart Coaching* gave me a good story to tell myself and a good story to tell others. It fulfilled my need for strength - a need I had not acknowledged.

I was also struggling with anxiety and sought possible explanations in highflying existential models. A friend of mine said: «*That's rubbish! The problem is lack of cash.*» Quite right. When I got a higher and steadier income my levels of anxiety went down considerably. I had not been in contact with my need for safety, but I was still struggling with the consequences.

If we have been closed off for a long time, or the pain and fear that led us to close off was significant, it can be difficult to open up again. Even when we find ourselves in a favourable situation – for example, in a relationship, we are not necessarily able to open up to love. First we must feel and transform the old pain that is blocking our access to the need.

I have personally experienced how intense the pain can be when the longing is awakened, but fulfillment is not coming. I really believed I had met the woman of my life – the pleasure in our meeting was greater than I had ever experienced and suddenly I wanted to have kids! Dreams and plans for the future were spinning on full throttle! Then she left for another. In such moments I see the need to close off, because the pain was greater than what I could contain.

Briefly summed up, we can say that we close off our contact with a need either because the fulfillment is not accessible in our current situation, or because we have

had painful experiences (traumas) related to that need –
either in childhood or later.

Fulfillment

It feels so good and beautiful when a deep need is met.
We are filled with a sense of fulfillment and joy that we
experience immediately and directly in our body.

As we get used to having our need met as part of our
everyday life, we don't feel it so strongly. However the
totality of who we are has been lifted to a higher quality
of life.

Overflowing

When the needs are filled up, we soon can feel how
they begin to overflow. We want to give, we want to
contribute and we want to help others. We don't need
so much in return, because giving by itself is so joyful.

When we live from a state of fullness, a higher order of
needs surfaces – the need to contribute and the need
to help others out of compassion. This has much in
common with the state called Bodhisattva in Buddhism.

THE SEVEN NEEDS

I. Safety

What is needed for each of us to feel safe varies greatly. Some people have a strong sense of security from childhood and do not need much to feel safe as an adult. Others basically feel unsafe and therefore need more to compensate for this.

The need for safety concerns survival.
Most of us need the most basic amenities to feel safe:

- *I have enough food*
- *I am in good health*
- *I feel safe in my body*
- *My economy is secure*
- *I have a good place to live*
- *There is peace/ political stability*
- *I live in a stable context*

II. Intimacy, enjoyment and sexuality

Intimacy is about the safe physical closeness that already began with our parents or caretakers. Without physical closeness we don´t survive as babies, nor as adults: intimacy is essential for our quality of life.

The need for enjoyment of food, for intimacy and for sex may appear quite different to each other, however they all share the direct sense enjoyment of bodily stimulus.

We experience immediate pleasure without the filter of understanding. Our body functions better when we enjoy the food we are eating, enjoy having a body, and enjoy being alive!

Lust, or horniness, is still taboo in most societies, probably because it can evoke such strong emotions and create intense conflicts when what is wanted is not attained. For example, the beautiful Helen of Troy was the trigger for a bloody and drawn out war in Antiquity. This is not the only war, on a big or small scale, caused by the frustrated longing to satisfy lust – caused by the pain and anger of not having this need met.

The need for intimacy is about enjoyment of our bodily senses. When my need for intimacy, enjoyment and sexuality are met, I can say that:

- *I enjoy food*
- *I feel good with physical closeness*
- *I enjoy my body receiving touch and caress*
- *I feel attractive and respect my body as it is*
- *I feel attracted to others and allow myself to feel the attraction*
- *I enjoy my own sexuality*
- *I enjoy my partner's enjoyment and sexuality*
- *I feel a deep connection with myself and my partner*

III. Strength

Power is a charged word, but if we turn it around and say that we don't want to be powerless it sounds better right away. As children we usually have very little power because decisions are made by others. But as we grow older we acquire ever more power over our own lives. Later on we influence other peoples' lives as well. Power over our own life is an essential need, but power over others can be misused. To develop a healthy sense of self, we need to find healthy boundaries between our own power and other people's power.

We derive strength from mastery; when we master a challenge we feel strong. To face our fear and still be able to overcome the obstacle strengthens us.

The need for strength is about being an independent individual. When my need for strength is met, I can say that:

- *I feel strong in my body*
- *I have a sense of personal strength and weight*
- *I am respected and appreciated*
- *I am proud of myself*
- *I have status in society*
- *I make my own choices*
- *I have control and mastery over life*
- *I have power and influence over my own life*
- *I have drive for action*
- *I take responsibility for my life*

IV. Love and belonging

Love is the greatest of all! If we have love in our life, everything else seems less important. As described above, love can contribute to fulfilling other needs, like safety, sexuality and strength, thus enabling our personal expression, enhancing our clarity and supporting our openness to something greater.

To love oneself is a prerequisite to truly love others. This love for oneself can be cultivated if not already present from childhood.

Love expresses itself in many different ways, or we can say there are many kinds of love, such as: the love of a parent for a child, love between friends, romantic love, love for family and community, and love for oneself.

**When my need for love and belonging is met,
I can say that**:

- *I love myself*
- *I love my family*
- *My family loves me*
- *I have a partner I love who loves me*
- *I have good and close friends*
- *I have family and friends who are there for me*
- *I help others when they need me*
- *I have a sense of belonging in a good community*
- *I give and receive*
- *I am seen and understood*
- *I contribute to my surroundings and to the world*

V. Expression

In this day and age we are exposed to more impressions than ever before – information coming from the outside in. However, we all have a need to express ourselves, to come from the inside out! We need to share with others what is true and right for us, and we have a need to create something from ourselves.

Spontaneity and play are ways to express who we are. There are many possible outlets of expression: a conversation with a friend, making food, writing, dancing, singing and all other forms of art. Just sitting alone on a bench in the park may be enough. These activities fulfill our everyday need for expression.

However, we might also long to create something great. We want to do something with our life, we have a vision or an idea we want to realise, or we have a gift we want to share with the world. There is a movement from the inside that wants to get out and become reality.

**When my need for expression is met,
I can say that**:

- *I say what is true to me*
- *I express truthfully who I am*
- *I express myself creatively*
- *I am spontaneous and playful*
- *What I think and want becomes true*
- *I unfold my vision*

VI. Clarity

The question about the meaning of life belongs to the need for clarity. We want to understand! Through the ages this has been the arena of myths and religions. In our time science and scientific mythologies have taken over much of this function. Regardless of which tradition we belong to, everything becomes so much easier and more satisfying when we have a story that brings all the threads together into one whole web – whether a chronological narrative, an ideology, a religion or a belief system. Such a story is further strengthened if we belong to a social context, for example a church or a political party. We all agree, that is, we are part of a collective group mind. Such collective stories give us answers that are intended to fulfill our need for clarity. It provides a certain satisfaction when we can say:

* *I understand the world*
* *I understand my place in the world*
* *I understand my purpose in the world*
* *I know how I should conduct myself*
* *I know what is right and wrong*

For me the answers given by collective systems were not enough. I realised early on that there were many conflicting answers. Through meditation I discovered another clarity that contains all contradictions – the awareness that experiences and sees all thoughts and beliefs. This form of clarity can also be called awake consciousness.

Do I believe every single thought that comes sailing through my head, or do I actively use my mind to think through different perspectives? Do I find myself inside a labyrinth, or do I see the maze from above? Am I reactive, or do I consciously make choices, accommodate my feelings and choose my expressions? Am I governed by old patterns or by a watchful presence in the moment?

**When this clarity is awake,
I can say that:**

- *I am the consciousness that contains everything I experience*
- *I contain my thoughts*
- *I contain my emotions*
- *I am aware and awake*
- *I have an overview*
- *I see many possibilities*
- *I learn and get new insights*
- *I understand and I am open for new understanding*
- *I make conscious choices*

This makes it possible for me to consciously choose through which understanding I see my experience. I can see the consequences of different ways of thinking. I can also find direction and meaning to what I do based on my inner calling, or what I want to give to the world – not what the world tells me to do to fit in.

VII. Wholeness

We all belong to a context. We are one link in a chain of generations, and we are a part of our culture and humanity. And, we are part of nature – even though many forget that in their everyday lives. No one lives independently of a larger context.

We have a need to know that we are part of the whole, that we are not separate and alone, but rather that we belong to a larger context. To have a sense of being outside of such a belonging can be very painful.

Some of us, spiritual or religious, believe or experience that we can get in touch with a higher consciousness. We experience this contact more strongly in meditation, prayer, religious rituals or when we are in nature.

The seventh need can be the door out of **the Wheel of Needs** – where we leave our individual needs behind, transcend ourselves and become like a drop in the ocean, inseparable from the One. This is freedom. When we experience this inner fullness, everything else falls away by itself.

When my need for wholeness has been met, I can say that:

- *I belong to a larger context*
- *I am in contact with something greater than myself*
- *I am in contact with my higher Self*
- *I am in contact with the source of life*
- *I am in contact with the Universe*
- *I am in contact with a higher consciousness*
- *I am in touch with God*
- *I am free*

NEEDS AND EMOTIONS

Joy and laughter, sorrow and sadness, jealousy and anger, fear and anxiety are reactions to needs that are met or not met. When needs are met, emotions arise. When needs are not met, emotions arise. When needs are closed off, we have no emotions. When needs are fulfilled, we find peace.

When the need for safety is not met, we get anxious or just plain scared. When the need is fulfilled, we experience peace in this aspect of life.

When we do not get physical closeness or intimacy, we experience that something is missing in life, a kind of emptiness or loneliness that can be difficult to pinpoint. When intimacy is a natural part of our life, the body relaxes.

When the need for sex is not met, the special yearning for this need shows up, namely lust. Frustrated lust can lead to anger or jealousy. Fulfillment gives pleasure and peace.

When the need for strength is not met, we feel small and worthless. This feeling is expressed as a contraction in the body and leads to fear of others, fear of social situations and self-deprecation.

Many feel small deep inside, but compensate by trying to make themselves big. They achieve to impress and create a mask of strength. This may express itself as childish pride or full-blown arrogance and self-aggrandisement. The need for strength has not found peace, and the person requires constant affirmation to avoid the feeling of inadequacy that lies within.

When the need for strength is fulfilled, we have a sense of self-respect and peace. We can find this self-respect by strengthening our relationship with our self, by following our own truth and by living in accordance with our own values.

To be proud of oneself feels good. If this pride is based on self-respect derived from following our truth, we strengthen our relationship to our self. If this pride is based on praise and affirmation from the outside world, it strengthens our dependence on the surroundings.

Love is not only a need, but is also experienced as an emotion. We feel warmth and kindness toward others. When we lose someone we hold dear, we mourn.

When we express ourselves truthfully, creatively and spontaneously we often feel joy! If we have kept our expression buried inside for a long time, then, when we finely let it out, we may feel sadness or grief at the lost opportunities, or anger towards those who held us back.

All needs can evoke a wide range of emotions depending on our personal story.

When we receive an important insight, we experience a special sense of fullness – a good feeling of having reached a new understanding. Such an experience can also evoke sadness, joy, excitement or relief. When we reach clarity it brings calm, a calm that can co-exist with, for example, sadness or joy.

To feel the longing for wholeness without completion is painful. When we wake up to the Whole, we are filled with bliss – a quiet and yet full joy.

A PATH TO FREEDOM

We can also fulfill ourselves internally. We can fill a need by being with it, acknowledging it, holding space for it and facing the pain we feel over what we don't have, what we long for. It is possible to see through and illuminate the structure of the needs, to see that it does not exist independently of our Self, our awake consciousness. We are our Self the source and origin of the need and its fulfillment. This is a path to freedom.

Once the needs have settled, it is easier to become aware of ourselves as awake presence. We also recognise this presence in other people even when they do not recognise it within themselves.

This fits nicely with something Joseph Campbell once wrote (*Joseph Campbell - A fire in the mind*, Larsen 2002, p. 103):

The absolute hangs like the moon above water, and the water is my very own soul. Winds of desire stir my soul and my vision of the absolute. My reflection of the moon, my notion of eternity is in splinters, but I desire only to see the truth, to reflect the moon and the winds die slowly...

In one´s attempt to silence «the winds of desire» one may come to close off rather than see through the structure of needs in an attempt to be more enlightened than one is. I think that is what happened to me. After years of meditation and pure living I experienced life as grey and meaningless, and it started to dawn on me that I had cut myself off from the pulse of life instead of connecting with the source. This is what I have been working on ever since - to acknowledge my needs and to find healthy and natural ways to fulfill them while being awake and present in my life.

www.ingramcontent.com/pod-product-compliance
Lightning Source LLC
Chambersburg PA
CBHW071547120626
46550CB00006B/2609